BRIEF INSTRUCTIONS UPO**... DEFEN(

for the true handling of all mann
with the four Grounds and the f...
Governors are left out in my Para... ...s, without the
knowledge of which no man can fight safe

By George Silver, Gentleman

This Scholler's Edition is based on the transcription of Sloan MS 376
by Cyril G. R. Matthey

Published 1898

Edited by Bruce Eaton

2014

First Printing 2014

ISBN 978-1-291-96576-6

www.medievalmartialarts.co.uk

'There is no manner of teaching comparable to the old ancient teachings, that is, first their quarters, then their wards, blows, thrusts, and breaking of thrusts, then their closes and grips, striking with the hilts, daggers, bucklers, wrestling, striking with foot or knee in the coddes, and all these are safely defended in learning perfectly of the grips. And this is ancient teaching, the perfect and most best teaching; and without this teaching, there shall never scholler be made able, do his uttermost, nor fight safe.'

George Silver

Paradoxes of Defence (1599)

'I suggest that sword *fighting* is not taught, and that it ought to be. Fencing should be encouraged to the utmost, but fighting should be regarded, as it was by Silver, as a distinct subject, and of much greater importance in the majority of cases.'

Cyril Matthey

The Works of George Silver (1898)

CONTENTS

A BRIEF INTRODUCTION

When George Silver [ca.1560s-1620s] published *Paradoxes of Defence* in 1599 a fashionable gentleman was not considered properly dressed without a rapier by his side and the enthusiasm for Continental rapier fencing amongst the upper echelons of English society was sweeping away traditional forms of swords and swordplay. The most celebrated fencing master in London prior to the publication of *Paradoxes* had been the Italian Vincentio Saviolo [d.1598/9]. Following in the footsteps of his compatriot Rocco Bonnetti [d.1587], Saviolo had moved to London in 1590 and opened a fencing school and in 1595, under the patronage of the Earl of Essex, published the first fencing manual to be composed in English, *Vincentio Saviolo, his practice, in two bookes, the first intreating of the use of the Rapier and Dagger, the second of Honor and honorable quarrels*. Like Bonnetti he had managed to side-step the monopoly enjoyed by the English Maisters of Defence by drawing his clientele from the noblemen and gentlemen of Court. Not only was this sophisticated Italian gentleman teaching a highly fashionable weapon, the steep fees made his school very exclusive. The English Maisters were traditionally drawn from the lower orders, as were the majority of their students, sniffily described by George Hale in his 1614 tract *The Private Schoole of Defence* as *'Butchers, Byt-makers, Shooe-makers, or Truncke-makers'*. Rather than rub shoulders, and trade blows, with these rude mechanics the young blades of Elizabethan London flocked to Saviolo.

This situation was an anathema to Silver. A staunch traditionalist in all matters martial and a connoisseur of the native fighting system *'having the perfect knowledge of all maner of weapôs, and being experiêced in all maner of fights'*, Silver leaves us in no doubt that he had long been a vocal critic of the rapier and the Italian fencing masters prior to publishing *Paradoxes*. He objected to the system being taught as lacking the four Governors, knowledge of the four Actions, understanding of the True and False Times and therefore it was dangerously flawed. Worse still, to Silver's mind at least, was the fact that the rapier was predominately a civilian weapon unsuited to the battlefield. The young gentlemen who studied the rapier as opposed to traditional arms would be of no service to their country when it came to war. So when Saviolo claimed that *'Englifhmen were ftrong men, but had no cunning, and they would go backe too much in their fight, which was a great difgrace vnto them'* Silver and his younger brother Toby challenged Saviolo and fellow Italian Jeronimo (who had formerly been Bonnetti's 'assistant' and is the probable translator of *DiGrassi, His True Arte of Defence*, published in English in 1594) to a public trial of arms pitching short swords and daggers against rapiers and poniards. The Silvers erected a scaffold at their own expense so *'he that went in his fight fafter back then he ought… fhould be in danger to breake his necke'*. The Italians resolutely ignored the challenge. Indeed, Saviolo continued to ignore challenges for the rest of his days causing Silver to remark that he was a better Christian than a fighter. Jeronimo did eventually pit his rapier and poniard against a short sword and dagger in a quarrel with a man named Cheese who *'with his Sword within two thruftes ran him* [Jeronimo] *into the bodie and flue him.'*

This enmity towards the Italian fencing masters and disdain for their system is the main thrust of *Paradoxes*, yet the book is far from the xenophobic rant that some fencing historians have characterised it as. Silver had equally hard words for the *'euill orders or customes in our English Fêce-Schooles'*. He criticised them for only teaching blows with swords and thrusts with rapiers, producing students that would not know how to break thrusts with one weapon or ward blows with the other. He also lamented that grips, closes, wrestling and strikes with the sword hilt, dagger or buckler were no longer commonly taught or tolerated within the schools. Silver notes that, *'as long as we barre anie maner of play in fchoole, we shall hardly make a good fcholler'*. Most controversially of all Silver claimed that the swords that were used for training were too long to be effective at close quarters; a charge that he had also levelled at rapiers.

It is clear that with *Paradoxes* Silver had succeeded in ruffling the feathers of many professional fencing masters. Joseph Swetnam [d.1621], the former fencing master to Prince Henry, appears to dedicate a whole chapter of his own fencing manual, *The Schoole of the Noble and Worthy Science of Defence* (1617), to rebutting Silver's arguments. Having previously proclaimed the rapier *as 'the finest & the comliest weapon that ever was used in England'* Swetnam goes on to describe Silver's beloved short sword as *'an idle weapon... to encounter against a long Sword and Dagger, or a long Rapier and Dagger'* and *'little better ten a tobacco-pipe, or a foxe-tayle'*. Indeed, he says that even describing the weapon is *'time ill spent'* and that he is only driven to it because *'Short swords are in use and worne of many that would leave them off if that they knew what an idle weapon it were'*. Were these gentlemen influenced by *Paradoxes*? It is perhaps telling that Swetnam goes on to state that *'...although that George Giller hath most highly commended that short sword & dagger, yet one Swallow maketh not a Summer, nor two Woodcocks a Winter.'*

And yet, significantly, *Paradoxes* seems to have failed to connect with a substantial number of young gentlemen seeking martial arts tuition. As Silver himself admits, to many readers *Paradoxes* was a *'dark riddle'*. Without having first attained a level of knowledge of the English system and the principles that underpin it Silver's self-evident truths were unintentionally esoteric. This, then, was the catalyst for *Bref Instructions Upô My Paradoxes of Defence,* which although unpublished in Silver's lifetime has become one of the most influential and widely read manuals in the Western martial arts canon. We are unsure when Silver began work on the manuscript, although it must have been after 1603 and the accession of James I & VI to the throne as Silver now refers to the *'ever victorious nation of great btytaine'* rather than to the *'most mightie nation of Englifhmen'* as he had done in *Paradoxes.* What makes the manuscript so unique is that from the very start Silver explains simply and with great clarity the underpinning theory, philosophy and mechanics of the system he is describing; his *Principles of the True Fight.* In the subsequent chapters the martial techniques described further illustrate these fundamentals. In short, Silver not only tells us 'how' but also 'why'.

The manuscript may very well have been lost to posterity had it not been discovered in the Manuscript Department of the British Museum in 1890 by Mr W. London. Convinced of the manuscript's veracity and of its practical value to swordsmen, London undertook the first transcription of the work and in 1894 presented this to Captain Alfred Hutton, a known authority on historical swordplay and author of *Cold Steel: A Practical Treatise on the Sabre* (1889), for his perusal. Hutton was much impressed, but when he tried to return the transcript he discovered that London had died and that he had been bequeathed the transcript for his own collection. It was some short time after this that Hutton brought the existence of *Bref Instructions* to the attention of his associate Colonel Cyril Matthey. Matthey, himself an expert fencer, believed that the swordplay taught in fencing schools was woefully inadequate when applied to a real battlefield situation especially *'against men of savage or barbarian races that Her Majesty's troops are so frequently sent to face'* (i.e. cultures still proficient in armed hand-to-hand combat). Recognising the similarities between Silver's short sword and the regulation infantry officer's sword of his own day, Matthey approved of the simplicity and efficiency of Silver's advice particularly in regards to defence, off-hand grappling and the use of the sword pommel for offensive strikes. He began work on his own transcription of *Bref Instructions* and in 1889 published it along with *Paradoxes* in a single volume.

Facsimile copies of Matthey's *The Works of George Silver* are now freely available on the internet and it is Matthey's transcription that has been used to prepare this book (look no further than www.sirwilliamhope.org/Library - a fantastic resource for historical fencing and boxing manuals hosted by the Linacre School of Defence). However, the layout of Matthey's book can often be problematic to the modern student as he lovingly crafted his edition to appear as it would have had it been published in Silver's day, complete with cramped type setting, archaic contractions and unconventional spelling. To further complicate matters Matthey's own marginalia assume the reader is already familiar with classical fencing terminology.

This *Scholler's Edition* has been designed with accessibility as its primary concern. It is not intended as an interpretation of Silver's work and Silver's language has not been altered. The spelling has been modernised for the sake of clarity. Similarly, the footnotes are there to provide an explanation of technical terms, expand on key concepts or include relevant supplementary material from *Paradoxes*. The page layout has been designed to make each of Silver's 'grounds' as digestible as possible with enough room for the reader's own notes. It is the editor's hope that this book will be covered in copious pencilled notes and highlighter pen, page corners will be creased to mark particular passages, that it will provide searching questions for your instructor to answer and well-thumbed and much abused it will nestle in your kitbag alongside your backsword and buckler.

Select Bibliography

Amberger, J.C. 1999 **The Secret History of the Sword: Adventures in Ancient Martial Arts** Multi-Media Books

Brown, T. 1997 **English Martial Arts** Anglo-Saxon Books

Hale, G. 1614 **The Private Schoole of Defence**

Hand, S. 2006 **English Swordsmanship: The True Fight of George Silver Vol. 1** The Chivalry Bookshelf

Hillyard, M.I. (ed.) 2011 **The Noble Science Vol. 1** Wyvern Media

Matthey, C.G.R. (ed.) 1898 **The Works of George Silver**

Saviolo, V. 1595 **Vincentio Saviolo, his practice, in two bookes, the first intreating of the use of the Rapier and Dagger, the second of Honor and honorable quarrels**

Swetnam, J. 1617 **The Schoole of the Noble and Worthy Science of Defence**

Wagner, P. (ed.) 2003 **Master of Defence: The Works of George Silver** Paladin Press

Wylde, Z. 1711 **The English Master of Defence**

To The Reader

For as much as in my Paradoxes of Defence I have admonished men to take heed of false teachers of defence, yet once again in these my Brief Instructions I do the like, because divers have written books treating of the noble science of defence, wherein they teach offence rather than defence, rather showing men thereby how to be slain than to defend themselves from the danger of their enemies, as we daily see to the great grief and overthrow of many brave gentlemen and gallants of our ever victorious nation of Great Britain. And therefore for the great love and care that I have for the well doing and preservation of my countrymen, seeing their daily ruin and utter overthrow of divers gallant gentlemen and others [who] trust only to that imperfect fight of that rapier, yes although they daily see their own overthrows and slaughter thereby, yet because they are trained up therein, they think and do fully persuade themselves that there is no fight so excellent and whereas amongst divers others their opinions that lead them to this error one of the chiefest is, because there be so many slain with these weapons and therefore they hold them so excellent, but these things do chiefly happen, first because their fight is imperfect for that they use neither the perfect grounds of the true fight, neither yet the four governors without which no man can fight safe, neither do they use such other rules which are required in the

i

right use of perfect defence, and also their weapons for the most part being of imperfect length, must by necessity make an imperfect defence because they cannot use them in due time and place, for had these valorous mlnded men the right perfection of the true fight with the short sword, and also of other weapons of perfect length, I know that men would come safer out of the field from such bloody banquets and that such would be their perfections herein, that it would save many hundred men's lives. But how should men learn perfection out of such rules as are nothing else but very imperfection itself? And as it is not fit for a man which desires the clear light of the day to go down into the bottom of a deep and dark dungeon, believing to find it there, so it is as impossible for men to find the perfect knowledge of this noble science where as in all their teachings everything is attempted and acted upon imperfect rules. For there is but one truth in all things, which I wish very heartily were taught and practiced here amongst us, and that those imperfect and murderous kinds of false fights might be by them abolished. Leave now to quaff and gull any longer of that filthy briny puddle, seeing you may now drink of that fresh and clear spring.

O that men for their defence would but give their mind to practice the true fight indeed and learn to bear true British wards for their defence, which if they had it in perfect practice, I speak it of my own knowledge that those imperfect Italian devices with rapier and poniard would be clean cast aside and of no account of all such as blind affections do not lead beyond the bounds of reason. Therefore for the very zealous and unfeigned love that I bear unto your high and Royal person my countrymen pitying their causes that so many brave men should be daily murdered and spoiled for want of true knowledge of this noble science and not as some imagine to be, only the excellence of the rapier fight, and where as my Paradoxes of Defence is to the most sort as a dark riddle in many things therein set down, therefore I have now this second time taken some pains to write these few brief instructions there upon whereby they may the better attain to the truth of this science and laying open here all such things as was something intricate for them to understand in my Paradoxes and therefore that I have the full perfection and knowledge of the perfect use of all manner of weapons, it does embolden me herein to write for the better instruction of the unskilful.

And I have added to these my brief instructions certain necessary admonitions which I wish every man not only to know but also to observe and follow, chiefly all such as are desirous to enter into the right usage and knowledge of their weapons and also I have thought it good to annex here unto my Paradoxes of Defence because in these my brief instructions, I have referred the reader to diverse rules therein set down.

This have I written for an infallible truth and a note of remembrance to our gallant gentlemen and others of our brave minded nation of Great Britain, which bear a mind to defend themselves and to win honour in the field by their actions of arms and single combats.

And know that I write not this for vainglory, but out of an entire love that I owe unto my native countrymen, as one who laments their losses, sorry that so great an error should be so carefully nourished as a serpent in their bosoms to their utter confusion, as of long time have been seen, whereas if they would but seek the truth herein they were easily abolished, therefore follow the truth and fly ignorance.

And consider that learning has no greater enemy than ignorance, neither can the unskilful ever judge the truth of my art to them unknown, beware of rash judgement and accept my labours as thankfully as I bestow them willingly, censure me justly, let no man despise my work herein causeless, and so I refer myself to the censure of such as are skilful herein and I commit you to the perfection of the almighty Jehovah.

Yours in all love and friendly affection

George Silver

ADMONITIONS TO THE GENTLEMEN AND BRAVE GALLANTS OF GREAT BRITAIN AGAINST QUARRELS AND BRAWLS WRITTEN BY GEORGE SILVER, GENTLEMAN

Whereas I have declared in my Paradoxes of Defence of the false teaching of the noble science of defence used here by the Italian fencers willing men therein to take heed how they trusted there unto with sufficient reasons and proofs why.

And whereas there was a book written by Vincento[1] an Italian teacher whose ill using practices and unskilful teaching were such that it has cost the lives of many of our brave gentlemen and gallants, the uncertainty of whose false teaching does yet remain to the daily murdering and overthrow of many, for he and the rest of them did not teach defence but offence, as it does plainly appear by those that follow the same imperfect fight according to their teaching or instructions by the orders from them proceeding, for be the actors that follow them never so perfect or skilful therein one or both of them are either sore hurt or slain in their encounters and fights, and if they allege that we use it not rightly according to the perfection thereof, and therefore cannot defend ourselves, to which I answer if themselves had any perfection therein, and that their teaching had been a truth, themselves would not have been

---

[1] *Vincentio Saviolo, his practice, in two bookes, the first intreating of the use of the Rapier and Dagger, the second of Honor and honorable quarrels* (1595)

beaten and slain in their fights, and using of their weapons, as they were.

And therefore I prove where a man by their teaching cannot be safe in his defence following their own ground of fight then is their teaching offence and not defence, for in true fight against the best no hurt can be done. And if both have the full perfection of true fight, then the one will not be able to hurt the other at what perfect weapon so ever.

For it cannot be said that if a man go to the field and cannot be sure to defend himself in fight and to come safe home, if God be not against him whether he fight with a man of skill or no skill it may not be said that such a man is Maister[2] of the noble science of defence, or that he has the perfection of true fight, for if both have the perfection of their weapons, if by any device, one should be able to hurt the other, there were no perfection in the fight of weapons, and this firmly hold in your mind for a general rule, to be the height and perfection of the true handling of all manner of weapons.

And also whereas that said Vincentio in that same book has written discourse of honour and honourable quarrels making many reasons to prove means and ways to enter the field and combat, both for the lie and other disgraces, all which diabolical devices tend only to

---

[2] Master

villainy and destruction as hurting, maiming and murdering or killing.

Animating the minds of young gentlemen and gallants to follow those rules to maintain their honours and credits, but the end thereof for the most part is either killing or hanging or both to the utter undoing and great grief of themselves, and their friends, but then too late to call it again. They consider not the time and place that we live in, nor do not thoroughly look into the danger of the law till it be too late, and for that in divers other countries in these things they have a larger scope than we have in these our days.

Therefore it behoves us not upon every abuse offered whereby our blood shall be inflamed, or our choler kindled presently with the sword or with the stab, or by force of arms to seek revenge, which is the proper nature of wild beasts in their rage so to do, being void of the use of reason, which thing should not be in men of discretion so much to degenerate, but he that will not endure an injury, but will seek revenge, then he ought to do it by civil order and proof, by good and wholesome laws, which are ordained for such causes, which is a thing far more fit and requisite in a place of so civil a government as we live in, then is the other, and who so follow these my admonitions shall be accounted as valiant a man as he that fights and far wiser. For I see no reason why a man should adventure his life and estate upon every trifle, but should rather put up divers abuses offered unto him, because it is agreeable to the laws of God and our country.

Why should not words be answered with words again, but if a man by his enemy be charged with blows then may he lawfully seek the best means to defend himself, and in such a case I hold it fit to use his skill and to show his force by his deeds, yet so, that his dealing be not with full rigour to the others confusion if possible it may be eschewed.

Also take heed how you appoint the field with your enemy publicly because our laws do not permit it, neither appoint to meet him in private sort lest you wounding him he accuse you of felony saying you have robbed him etc. Or he may lay company closely to murder you and then report he did it himself valiantly in the field.

Also take heed of thy enemy's stratagems, lest he find means to make you look aside upon something, or cause you to show whether you have on a privy coat, and so when you look from him, he hurt or kill you.

Take not arms upon every light occasion, let not one friend upon a word or trifle violate another but let each man zealously embrace friendship, and in turn not familiarity into strangeness, kindness into malice, nor love into hatred, nourish not these strange and unnatural alterations.

Do not wickedly resolve one to seek to the other's overthrow, do not confirm to end thy malice by fight because for the most part it ends by death.

Consider when these things were most used in former ages they fought not so much by envy the ruin and destruction one of another, they never took trial by sword but in the defence of innocence to maintain blotless honour.

Do not upon every trifle make an action of revenge, or of defiance.

Go not into the field with thy friend at his entreaty to take his part but first know the manner of the quarrel how justly or unjustly it grew, and do not therein maintain wrong against right, but examine the cause of the controversy, and if there be reason for his rage to lead him to that mortal resolution.

Yet be the cause never so just, go not with him never further nor suffer him to fight if possible it may be by any means to be otherwise ended and will him not to enter into so dangerous an action, but leave it till necessity requires it.

And this I hold to be the best course for it is foolishness and endless trouble to cast a stone at every dog that barks at you. This noble science is not to cause one man to abuse another injuriously but to use it in their necessities to defend them in their just causes and to maintain their honour and credits.

Therefore fly all rashness, pride and doing of injury all foul faults and errors herein, presume not upon this, and thereby to think it lawful to offer injury to any, think not yourself invincible, but consider that often a very wretch has killed a tall man, but he that has humanity, the more skilful he is in this noble science, the more humble, modest and virtuous he should show himself both in speech and action, no liar, no vaunter nor quarreller, for these are the causes of wounds, dishonour and death.

If you talk with great men of honourable quality with such chiefly have regard to frame your speeches and answer so reverent, that a foolish word, or forward answer give no occasion of offence for often they breed deadly hatred, cruel murders and extreme ruins etc.

Ever shun all occasions of quarrels, but martial men chiefly generals and great commanders should be excellent skilful in the noble science of defence, thereby to be able to answer quarrels, combats and challenges in defence of their prince and country.

Vale

X

CHAPTER 1

The four grounds or principles of the true fight at all manner of weapons are these four, viz.

1. Judgement   2. Distance   3. Time   4. Place

The reason whereof these four grounds or principles be the first and chiefest, are the following, because through Judgement, you keep your Distance, through Distance you take your Time, through Time you safely win or gain the Place of your adversary, the Place being won or gained you have time safely either to strike, thrust, ward, close, grip, slip or go back, in which time your enemy is disappointed to hurt you, or to defend himself, by reason that he has lost his true Place, the reason that he has lost his true Place is by the length of Time through the number of his feet[3], to which he is of necessity driven to that will be agent[4].

---

[3] By keeping your distance your opponent has had to step in towards you in order to attack allowing you to react in a quicker time and winning you the Place (see *true and false times, below*).

[4] Agent = aggressive protagonist who presses in without first gaining the Place.   Here Silver warns against ever being the agent. In his 'invincible conclusion' to *Paradoxes of Defence* Silver states, '...*whosoever shall think or find himself in his fight too weak for the agent, or patient agent, and therefore, or by reason of his drunkenness, or unreasonable desperation shall press within the half sword, or desperately run in of purpose to give hurt, or at least for taking one hurt, to give another, shall most assuredly*

The four governors are those that follow.

1. Judgement   2. Measure   3. Press In   4. Fly Backward

1.   The first governor is Judgement which is to know when your
     adversary can reach you, and when not, and when you can do
     the like to him, and to know by the goodness or badness of his
     lying, what he can do, and when and how he can perform it.

2.   The second governor is Measure. Measure is the better to
     know how to make your space true to defend yourself, or to
     offend your enemy.

3.   The third and fourth governors [are] a twofold mind when you
     press in on your enemy, for as you have a mind to go forward...

4.   ...so you must have at that instant a mind to fly backward upon
     any action that shall be offered or done by your adversary.

---

*be in great danger of death or wounds, and the other shall still be safe and
go free.'*

As well as observing the grounds and governors it is equally important to understand the True Times and the False Times. Moving in a True Time allows you act or react in the quickest time possible, while moving in a False Time creates openings that your opponent can exploit. The following text is taken from Paradoxes of Defence *Chapter 18 and presents the Times in descending order.*

The names and numbers of times appertaining unto fight both true and false.

There are eight times, whereof four are true, and four are false:

The true times be these.

The time of the hand.

The time of the hand and body.

The time of the hand, body and foot.

The time of the hand, body and feet.

The false times be these.

The time of the foot.

The time of the foot and body.

The time of the foot, body and hand.

The time of the feet, body and hand.

Thus have I thought good to separate and make known the true times from the false, with the true wards thereto belonging, that thereby the rather in practicing of weapons, a true course may be taken for the avoiding of errors and evil customs, and speedy attaining of good habit or perfect being in the true use and knowledge of all manner of weapons.

CHAPTER 2

Certain general rules which must be observed in the perfect use of all kind of weapons.

1. First when you come into the field to encounter with your enemy, observe well the scope, evenness and unevenness of your ground, put yourself in readiness with your weapon, before your enemy comes within distance, set the sun in his face traverse if possible you can still remembering your governors.

2. Let all your lying be such as shall best like yourself, ever considering out what fight your enemy charges you, but be sure to keep your distance, so that neither head, arms, hands, body, nor legs be within his reach, but that he must first of necessity put in his foot or feet, at which time you have the choice of 3 actions by which you may endanger him and go free yourself.

   i)   The first is to strike or thrust at him, at that instant when he has gained you the place by his coming in

ii) The second is to ward, and after to strike him or thrust from it, remembering your governors[5]

iii) The third is to slip a little back and to strike or thrust after him

But ever remember that in the first motion of your adversary towards you, that you slide a little back so shall you be prepared in due time to perform any of the 3 actions aforesaid by disappointing him of his true place[6] whereby you shall safely defend yourself and endanger him.

Remember also that if through fear or policy, he strike or thrust short, and therewith go back, or not go back, follow him upon your twofold governors[7], so shall your ward and slip be performed in like manner as before, and you yourself still be safe.

3. Keep your distance and suffer not your adversary to win or gain the place of you, for if he shall so do, he may endanger to hurt or kill you.

---

[5] Silver's writing is often credited with being the earliest source that advocates 'Parry and Riposte' fencing. Chapter 5 deals exclusively with riposting from a ward.
[6] By slipping back you have moved the intended target.
[7] Governors 3 and 4 – Press In and Fly Backwards.

Know that the place is, when one may strike or thrust home without putting in of his foot.[8]

It may be objected against this last ground, that men do often strike and thrust at the half sword and yet the same is perfectly defended, where to I answer that the defence is perfectly made by reason that the warder has his true space[9] before the striker or thruster is in force or entered into his action.

Therefore always do prevent both blow and thrust, the blow by true space[10], and the thrust by narrow space[11] that is true crossing it before the same come into their full force, otherwise the hand of the agent being as swift as the hand of the patient[12], the hand of the agent being the first mover, must of necessity strike of thrust that part of the patient which shall be struck or thrust at because the time of the hand to the time of the hand, being of like swiftness the first mover has the advantage.

---

[8] Time of the hand or Time of the hand and body.
[9] Space is the distance the sword blade has to travel from one position to another.
[10] A weapon position from where you can ward a blow in due time.
[11] A weapon position that is in line with your opponent's thrust allowing you to ward before the thrust is in full force.
[12] Patient or Patient Agent = defensive protagonist fighting according to the Principles.

4. When your enemy shall press upon you, he will be open in one place or other, both at single and double weapon[13], or at least he will be too weak in his ward upon such pressing, then strike or thrust at such open or weakest part that you shall find nearest.[14]

5. When you attempt to win the place, do it upon guard, remembering your governors, but when he presses upon you and gains you the place, then strike or thrust at him in his coming in.

Or if he shall strike or thrust at you, then ward it, and strike or thrust at him from your ward, and fly back instantly according to your governors, so shall you escape safely, for that the first motion of the feet backward is more swift, than the first motion of the feet forward, where by your regression will be more swift, than his course in progression to annoy you, the reason is, that in the first motion of his progression his number and weight is greater than yours are, in your first motion of your regression, nevertheless all men know that the continual

---

[13] Single weapon – a single sword for example. Double weapon – sword and buckler for example
[14] The first of the 3 actions mentioned in ground 2.

course of the feet forward is more swift than the continual course of the feet backwards.[15]

6. If your enemy lies in variable fight[16], and strikes or thrusts at you then be sure to keep your distance and strike or thrust at such open part of him as are nearest unto you, viz., at the hand, arm, head or leg of him, and go back with all.

7. If two men fight at the variable fight, and if within distance, they must both be hurt, for in such fight they cannot make a true cross, not have time truly to judge, by reason that the swift motion of the hand, being a swifter mover, then the [hand] deceives the eye, at what weapon so ever you shall fight with all, as in my *Paradoxes of Defence* in the [4th] chapter thereof does appear.

8. Look to the grip of your enemy[17], and upon his slip take such ward as shall best fit your hand, from which ward strike or thrust, still remembering your governors.

---

[15] When you initially fly backwards after attacking from the Place you are moving too fast for your opponent to catch you before you have regained Distance. However, if you continue to fly directly backwards within a few steps your opponent will have caught up with you and as you are both moving your feet you have lost the advantage of Distance and Time

[16] See Chapter 3 ground 4

[17] A grip is a grappling move to take control of your opponent's weapon or to bind their sword arm – see Chapter 6

11

9.   If you can indirect your enemy at any kind of weapon, then you have the advantage, because he must move his feet to direct himself again, and you in the meantime may strike or thrust at him, and fly out fast, before he can offer anything at you, his time will be so long.[18]

10. When you shall ward blow and thrust, made at your right or left part, with any kind of weapon, remember to draw your hind foot a little circularly, from that part to which the same shall be made, whereby you shall make your defence the more perfect, and shall stand the more apt to strike or thrust from it.[19]

---

[18] To misdirect. This refers to either moving the target area, as in Chapter 4 ground 7 for example, or forcing your opponent's weapon aside, as in Chapter 4 ground 21 for example. It can also refer to physically moving your opponent off line, as in Chapter 6 ground 4.

[19] For example if you ward a strike to your left side draw your back foot to the right as you ward. This is mechanically the strongest position to resist the force of your opponent's blow. Note that this moves your head and body from their original position and away from your opponents attack. It has also changed the line of your attack. This opens up targets for your riposte and when you fly backwards your opponent will have to realign them self before pressing in for another attack.

CHAPTER 3

A declaration of all the 4 general fights to be used with the sword at double or single, long or short, and with certain particular rules to them annexed.

1. **Open fight** is to carry your hand and hilt aloft above your head, either with point upright, or point backward, which is best, yet use that which you shall find most apt, to strike, thrust, or ward.

2. **Guardant fight** in general is of two sorts, the first is true guardant fight, which is either perfect or imperfect.

   The perfect is to carry your hand and hilt above your head with your point down towards your left knee, with your sword blade somewhat near your body, not bearing out your point, but rather declining in a little towards your said knee, that your enemy cross not your point and so hurt you, stand bolt upright in his fight, and if he offers to press in then bear your head and body a little backward.

   The imperfect is when you bear your hand and sword hilt perfect high above your head, as aforesaid but leaning or stooping forward with your body and thereby your space will be too wide on both sides to defend the blow struck at the left side of your head or too wide to defend a thrust from the right side of the body.

Also it is imperfect, if you bear your hand and hilt as aforesaid, bearing your point too far out from your knee, so that your enemy may cross, or strike aside your point, and thereby endanger you.

The second is the bastard guardant fight which is to carry your hand and hilt below your head, breast high or lower with your point downward toward your left foot, this bastard guardant ward is not to be used in a fight, except it be to cross your enemy's ward at his coming in to take the grip of him or such advantage, as in divers places of the sword fight is set forth.

3. **Close fight** is when you cross at the half sword either above at the forehand ward that is with the point high, and hand and hilt low, or at the true or bastard guardant ward with both your points down.

Close is all manner of fights wherein you have made a true cross at the half sword, with your space very narrow and not crossed is also close fight.

4. **Variable fight** is all other manner of lying not here before spoken of, whereof these four that follow are the chiefest of them.

    i)   **Stocata**: which is to lie with your right leg forward, with your sword or rapier hilt back on the outside of your right thigh with your point forward to ward your enemy, with your dagger in your hand extending your hand towards the point of your rapier, holding your dagger with the point upright with narrow space between your rapier blade, and the nails of your dagger hand, keeping your rapier point back behind your dagger hand if possible.

    Or he may lie wide below under his dagger with his rapier point down towards his enemy's foot, or with his point forward without his dagger.

    ii)   **Imbrocata**: is to lie with your hilt higher than your head, bearing your knuckles upward, and your point depending toward your enemy's face or breast.

iii)   **Mountanta**: is to carry your rapier pommel in the palm of your hand resting it on your little finger with your hand below and so mounting it up aloft, and so to come in with a thrust upon your enemy's face or breast, as of out of the Imbrocata.

iv)   **Passata**: is either to pass with the Stocata, or to carry your sword or rapier hilt by your right flank, with your point directly against your enemy's belly, with your left foot forward, extending forth your dagger hand with the point of your dagger forward as you do your sword, with narrow space between your sword and dagger blade, and so make your passage upon him.

Also any other kind of variable fight or lying whatsoever a man can devise not here expressed, is contained under this fight.

CHAPTER 4

Of the short single sword fight against the like weapon[20]

1. If your enemy lie aloft, either in the open or true guardant fight, and then strike at the left side of your head or body your best ward to defend yourself, is to bear it with true guardant ward, and if he strike and come in to the close, or to take the grip of you you may then safely take the grip of him as it appears in the chapter of the grip. [Chapter 6]

2. But if he do strike and not come in, then instantly upon your ward, uncross and strike him either on the right or left side of the head, and fly out instantly.

3. If you bear this with forehand ward, be sure to ward his blow, or keep your distance, otherwise he shall deceive you with

---

[20] Silver's *short sword* is a basket hilted backsword, a cut and thrust sword with a triangular cross section and a single cutting edge. The techniques described can be applied equally to the broadsword. Zach Wylde in *The English Master of Defence* (1711) presents his techniques for both types of sword as one and the same. In *Paradoxes of Defence* Chapter 15 Silver says; *'The best lengths for perfect teaching of the true fight... to accord with the true stature of all men, are these. The blade to be a yard and an inch [94cm] for mean statures, and for men of tall statures, a yard and three or four inches [99cm - 1.1m], and no more.'* The reason for these lengths are elaborated on in *Paradoxes of Defence* Chapter 19; *'If the sword be longer, you can hardly uncross without going back with your feet. If shorter you can hardly make a true cross without putting in of your feet, which times are too long to answer the time of the hand.'*

every false[21], still endangering your head, face, hand, arms, body, and bending knee, with blow or thrust. Therefore keep well your distance, because you can very hardly discern (being within distance), by which side of your sword he will strike, nor at which of those parts aforesaid, because of the swift motion of the hand deceives the eye.

4. If he lie aloft and strike as aforesaid at your head, you may endanger him if you thrust at his hand, hilt or arm, turning your knuckles downward, but fly back with all in the instant that you thrust.

5. If he lie aloft as aforesaid, and strike aloft at the left side of your head, if you will ward his blow with forehand ward, then be sure to keep your distance, except he comes so certain that you be sure to ward his blow, at which time if he comes in withal, you may endanger him from that ward, either by blow, thrust or grip.[22]

6. If he lie aloft and you lie low with your sword in the variable fight, then if you offer to ward his blow made at your head, with true guardant ward your time will be too long due in time

---

[21] Feint

[22] Only attempt this ward if you are sure that your opponent's attack isn't a feint, otherwise slip back. This is a reiteration of advice given in ground 3.

to make a sure ward[23], for that it is better to bear it with the forehand ward, but be sure to keep your distance, to make him come in with his feet, whereby his time will be too long to do that he intended.

7. If two men fight both upon open fight, he that first breaks his distance, if he attempt to strike at the other's head, shall be surely struck on the head himself, if the patient agent strike there at his coming in, and slip a little back withal, for that sliding back makes an indirection, whereby your blow crosses his head, and makes a true ward for your own, this will that be, because the length of time in his coming in.

8. Also if two fight upon open fight, it is better for the patient to strike home strongly at the agent's head, when the said agent shall press upon him to win the place than to thrust, because the blow of the patient is not only hurtful to the agent, but also makes a true cross to defend his own head.

9. If he charge you aloft, out of the open or true guardant fight, if you answer him with the imperfect guardant fight, with your body leaning forward, your space will be too wide on both sides to make a true ward in due time, and your arm and body

---

[23] The slow time is due to the wide space between hand positions.

will be too near unto him, so that with the bending of his body with the time of hand and foot, he may take the grip of you.

But if you stand upright in true guardant fight, then he cannot reach to take the grip of you, nor otherwise to offend you if you keep your distance, without putting in of his foot or feet wherein his number will be too great, and so his time will be too long, and you in that time may by putting in of your body take the grip of him, if he press to come in with using only your hand, or hand and foot, and there upon you may strike or thrust with your sword and fly out withal according to your governors, see more of this, in the chapter of the grip. [Chapter 6]

10. If he will still press forcibly aloft upon you, charging you out of the open fight or the true guardant fight, intending to hurt you in the face or head, or to take the grip of you, against such a one, you must use both guardant and open fight, whereby upon every blow or thrust that he shall make at you, you may from your wards, strike or thrust him on the face, head, or body as it appears more at large in the 5th chapter of these my instructions.

11. If you fight with one that stands only upon his guardant fight or if he seeks to come in to you by the same fight, then do you

strike and thrust continually at all manner of open places that shall cone nearest unto you, still remembering your governors, so shall he continually be in danger, and often wounded, and wearied in that kind of fight, and you shall be safe, the reason is, he is a certain mark to you, and you are an uncertain mark to him.

And further because he ties himself unto one kind of fight only, he shall be wearied for want of change of lying, and you by reason of many changes shall not only fight at ease, and much more brave, but you have likewise four fights to his one, to wit, guardant, open, closed and variable fight, to his guardant only, therefore that fight only is not to be stood upon or used.

12. But if all this will not serve, and although he has received many wounds, will continually run to come in, and forcibly break your distance, then may you safely take the grip of him, and hurt him at your pleasure with your sword, as appears in the chapter of the grip [Chapter 6], and he can neither hurt nor take the grip of you, because the number of his feet are too many, to bring his hand in place in due time, for such a one ever gains you the place, therefore be sure to take your time herein.

e like sort may you do at sword and dagger, or sword and ckler, at such time as I say, that you may take the grip at the single sword fight, you may then instead of the grip, soundly strike him with your buckler on the head or stab him with your dagger and instantly either strike up his heels[24] or fly out, and as he likes a cooling card to his hot brain, *sic fit*[25], so let him come for another.

13. If two fight and both lie upon the true guardant fight and that one of them will need seek to win the half sword by pressing in, that may you safely do, for upon that fight the half sword may safely be won, but he that first comes in must first go out, and that presently, otherwise his guard will be too wide above to defend his head, or if fit for that defence, then will it be too wide underneath to defend that thrust from his body which things the patient agent may do, and fly out safe, and that agent cannot avoid it, because the moving of his feet makes his ward unequal to defend both parts in due time, but the one or the other will be deceived and in danger, for he being agent upon his first entrance his time (by reason of the number of his feet) will be too long, so that the patient agent may first enter into his action, and the agent must be of force an after doer, and therefore cannot avoid this offense aforesaid.

---

[24] trip
[25] *LATIN* – thus becomes

14. If he come in to encounter the close and grip upon the bastard guardant ward, then you may cross his blade with yours upon the like guardant ward also, and as he comes in with his feet and have gained you the place, you may presently uncross and strike him a sound blow on the head, and fly out instantly, wherein he cannot offend you by reason of his lost time, nor defend himself upon the uncrossing, because his space is too wide whereby his time will be too long in due time to prevent your blow, this may you do safely.

15. If he comes in upon the bastard guardant ward, bearing his hilt lower than his head, or but breast high or lower, then strike him soundly on the head which thing you may easily do, because his space is too wide in due time to ward the same.

16. If your enemy charge you upon his Stocata fight, you may lie variable with large distance and uncertain with your sword and body at your pleasure, yet so you may strike, thrust or ward, and go forth and back as occasion is, to take the advantage of this coming in, whether he does it out of the Stocata, or Passata, which advantage you shall sure to have, if you observe this rule and be not too rash in your actions, by reason that the number of his feet will be great, and also because when those two fights are met together, it is hard to make a true cross,

therefore without large distance be kept of them, commonly they are both hurt or slain, because in narrow distance their hands have free course and are not tied to the time of the foot, by which swlft motion of the hand the eye is deceived, as you may read more at large in the [4th] chapter of my Paradoxes of Defence.

You may also use this fight, against the long sword, or long rapier, single or double.

Upon this ground some shallow witted fellow may say, if the patient must keep large distance then he must be driven to go back still, to which I answer that in the continual motion and traverses of his ground he is to traverse circular wise, forwards, backwards, upon the right hand, and upon the left hand, the which traverses are a certainty to be used within himself, and not to be prevented by the agent, because the agent comes on upon an uncertain mark, for when he thinks to be sure of his purpose, the patient is sometimes on the one side, and sometimes on the other side, sometimes too far back, and sometimes too near, so still the agent must use the number of his feet which will be too long to answer the hand of the patient agent, and it cannot be denied but the patient agent by reason of his large distance, still sees what the agent does in his coming, but the agent cannot see what the other does, till the patient agent be into his action, therefore too late for him either to hurt the patient, or in due time to defend himself, because he entered into his action upon the knowledge of the patient, but he knows not what the patient agent will do till it be too late.

17. If the agent say that then he will stand fast upon some sure guard and sometimes moving and traversing his ground, and keep large distance as the patient does, to which I answer, that when two men shall meet that have both the perfection of their weapons, against the best no hurt can be done, otherwise if by any device one should be able to hurt the other, then were there were there no perfection in the use of weapons, this perfection of fight being observed, prevents both close fight, and all manner of closes, grips and wrestling and all manner of such devices whatsoever.[26]

18. Also if charges you upon his Stocata, or any other lying after that fashion, with his point low and large [s]paced, then lie you aloft with your hand and hilt above your head, either true guardant, or upon the open fight, then he cannot reach you if

---

[26] Both protagonists are keeping perfect Distance and denying each other the Place and neither will press in without first winning the Place in accordance with the grounds and governors and so neither can be hurt. This also demonstrates the importance of self-composure and patience.

you keep your distance without putting in his foot or feet, but you may reach him with the time of your hand, or with the time of your hand and body, or of the hand, body and foot, because he has already put in his body within your reach and has gained you the place, and you are at liberty and without his reach, till he put in his foot or feet , which time is too wide in that place to make a ward in due time to defend his head, arms and hand, one of which will be always within your reach.

Note still in this that your weapons be both short of the equal and convenient length of the short sword.[27]

19. If out of his variable fight he strikes at the right or left side of the head or body, then your best ward is to bear with the forehand ward, otherwise your space will be too wide and too far to make your ward in due time.[28]

20. If he lies variable after the manner of the Passata then if you lie aloft as is above said, you have the advantage, because he that lies variable cannot reach home, at head, hand or arm, without putting in his foot or feet, and therefore it cannot be denied, but that he that plays aloft, has still the time of the hand to the

---

[27] This technique is not to be used against an opponent armed with a long sword or long rapier.

[28] This ground assumes both agent and patient agent are in variable fight with the hand and hilt low

time of the foot, which fight being truly handled is advantage invincible.[29]

21. If he lies variable upon the Imbrocata, then make a narrow space with your point upward, and suddenly if you can cross his point with your blade, put aside his point strongly with your sword and strike or thrust at him, and fly out instantly, ever remembering your governors that he deceive you not in taking his point.[30]

22. If he strike or thrust at your leg or lower part out of any fight, he shall not be able to reach the same unless you stand large paced with bending knee[31], or unless he comes in with his foot or feet, the which if he shall so do, then you may strike or thrust at his arm or upper part for then he puts them into the place gaining you the place whereby you make strike home upon him and he cannot reach you.

---

[29] Here Silver is reiterating the advice given in ground 18

[30] A sword blade may be divided into two parts, strong and weak, which refers to the amount of force that part of the blade can resist when crossed by another blade. From the hilt to the centre of the blade is strong and from the centre of the blade to the point is weak. The point is the weakest, or least resistant, part of the whole blade and if it can be crossed is relatively easy to beat aside. For this reason it is important to avoid warding strikes with the weak part of a backsword blade.

[31] A wide stance with your weight forward.

But if he stands large paced with bending knee, then win the place and strike home freely at his knee, and fly back therewith.

23. If he comes to the close fight with you and that you are both crossed aloft at the half sword with both your points upward, then if he comes in withal in his crossing bear strongly your hand and hilt over his wrist, close by his hilt, putting in over at the backside of his hand and hilt pressing down his hand and hilt strongly and suddenly, in your entering in, and so thrust your hilt in his face, or strike him upon the head with your sword, and strike up his heels, and fly out.[32]

24. If you are both so crossed at the bastard guardant ward, and if he then presses in, then take the grip of him as is shown in the chapter of the grip.

Or with your left hand or arm, strike his sword blade strongly and suddenly toward your left side by which means you are uncrossed, and he is discovered, then may you thrust him in the body with your sword and fly out instantly, which thing cannot be avoided, neither can he offend you.

---

[32] This technique is reiterated in Chapter 6 ground 6.

Or being so crossed, you may suddenly uncross and strike him upon the head and fly out instantly which thing you may safely do and go out free.

25. If you be both crossed at the half sword with his point up and your point down in the true guardant ward, then if he press to come in, then either take the grip of him, as in the chapter of the grip, or with your left and or arm, strike out his sword blade towards your left side as aforesaid, and so you may thrust him in the body with your sword and fly out instantly.

26. Do you never attempt to close or come to grip at these weapons unless it be upon the slow motion or disorder of your enemy,

But if he will close with you, then you may take the grip of him safely at his coming in, for he that first by strong pressing in adventuring the close loses it, and is in great danger, by reason that the number of his feet are too great, whereby his time will be too long, in due time to answer the hand of the patient agent, as in the chapter of the grip does plainly appear.

27. Always remembering if you fight upon the variable fight that you ward upon the forehand ward, otherwise your space will

be too wide in due time to make a true guardant ward, to defend yourself.[33]

28. If you fight upon open fight, or true guardant fight, never ward upon forehand ward for then your space will be too wide also, in due time to make a sure ward.

29. If he lies aloft with his point towards you, after the manner of the Imbrocata, then make your space narrow with your point upward and put by his point, and strike or thrust as aforesaid but be sure herein to keep your distance, that he deceive you not in taking of his point.[34]

---

[33] This is a reiteration of advice given in ground 6
[34] This is a reiteration of advice given in ground 18

CHAPTER 5

**Of divers advantages that you may take by striking from your
ward at the sword fight**

1. If your enemy strikes at the right side of your head, you lying
    true guardant, then put your hilt a little down, mounting your
    point, so that your blade may cross athwart your face, so shall
    you make a true ward for the right side of your head, from
    which ward you may instantly strike him on the right or left
    side of the head, or turn down your point, and thrust him in
    the body, or you may strike him on the left side of the body, or
    on the outside of his left thigh.

    Or you may strike him on the outside of the right thigh, one of
    those he cannot avoid if he not fly back instantly upon his
    blow, because he knows not which of these the patient agent
    will do.

2. If you lie upon your true guardant ward, and he strikes at the
    left side of your head, you have the choice from your ward to
    strike him from it, on the right side or left side of the head, or
    to turn down your point, and thrust him in the body, or you
    may strike him on the outside of the right or left thigh, for the

reason above said in the last rule, except he fly out instantly upon his blow.

3. If he charge you upon the open or true guardant fight, if you will answer him with the like, then keep your distance, and let your gathering be always in that fight to ward his right side so shall you with your sword choke up any blow that he can make at you, from the which ward you may strike him on the right or left side of the head, or thrust him in the body.

    But if he thrust at your face or body, then you may out of your guardant fight break it downward with your sword bearing your point strongly towards your right side, from the which breaking of his thrust you may likewise strike him from the right or left side of the head, or thrust him in the body.

4. If you meet with one that cannot strike from his ward, upon such a one you may both double[35] and false[36] and so deceive him, but if he be skilful you must not do so, because he will be still so uncertain in his traverse that he will still prevent you of time and place, so that when you think to double and false, you shall gain him the place and there upon he will be before

---

[35] Consecutive attacks at the same target
[36] Feint

you in his action, and in your coming he will still endanger you.[37]

5. If you fight upon the variable fight, and that you receive a blow with forehand ward, made at the right side of your head or body, you have the choice of eight offensive actions from that ward, the first to strike him on the right side, either on the head, shoulder, or thigh, or to thrust him in the body, or to strike him on the left side either on the head, shoulder or thigh, or to thrust him in the body, the like may you do if he strike ever at your left side, as is above said, if you bear it with your forehand ward.

6. In this forehand ward keep your distance, and take heed that he deceives you not with the downright blow at your head out of his open fight, for being within distance the swift motion of

---

[37] *Brief Instructions* is unusual in that Silver gives no directions for performing a false. In contrast his contemporary Joseph Swetnam, *The Schoole of the Noble and Worthy Science of Defence* (1617), and later authors such as Zach Wilde, *The English Master of Defence* (1711), spend much time over describing false play. As a false is performed by the Agent, breaking Distance with a feint attack in order to gain the Place, we can see why Silver would disapprove. Silver says; '*Our ploughmen have mightily prevailed... against Maisters of Defence both in schools and countries, that have taken upon them to stand upon school-tricks and juggling gambols: whereby it grew into common speech among the countrymen, "Bring me to a fencer, I will bring him out of his fence tricks with good downright blows".' (Paradoxes of Defence* Chapter 1)

the hand may deceive your eye, because you know not by which side of your sword his blow will come.

7. Also see that he deceive you not upon any false offering to strike at the one side, and when thereby you have turned your point aside, then to strike on the other side, but if you keep distance you are free from that, therefore still in all your actions remember your governors.

8. If he will do nothing but thrust, answer him as it is set down in the 16th ground of the short sword fight and also in divers places of the 8th chapter.

9. Also consider if he lie at the thrust upon the Stocata or Passata, and you have no way to avoid him, except you can cross his sword blade with yours, and so indirect his point, therefore keep narrow space upon his point, and keep well your distance in using your traverses.

    But if he puts forth his point so that you may cross it with forehand ward, for if you watch for his thrust then lie upon forehand ward with you point a little up. If he lie with his pointed mounted, and if you single your thrust upon the outside of your sword to ward your right side, or back of your sword hand, strike or bear his point out towards your right side, and there upon putting forward your body and left foot circular wise toward his right side you may strike him upon his sword arm, head, face or body.

Or if you take it on the inside of your sword blade to ward your left side then with your sword put by his point strongly and suddenly towards your left side, drawing your left foot circular wise back behind the heal of your right foot, and strike him on the inside of his sword hand or arm or on the head, face, or body, and fly out according to your governors.

This may you use against the sword and dagger long or short, or rapier and poniard, or sword and buckler.

10. Also remember if he has a long sword and you a short sword, ever to make your space so narrow, that you may always break his thrust before that be in force if possible you may, and also to keep large distance whether he charge you out of the Stocata, Passata, or Imbrocata, etc.

Of this you may see more at large in the 8th chapter.

CHAPTER 6

The manner of certain grips and closes to be used at the single short sword fight etc.[38]

1. If he strike aloft at the left side of your head, and run in withal to take the close or grip of you, then ward it guardant, and enter in with your left side putting in your left hand, on the inside of his sword arm, near his hilt, bearing your hand over his arm, and wrap in his hand and sword under your arm, as he comes in, wrestling his hand and sword close to your body turning back your right side from him, so shall he not be able to reach your sword, but you shall still have it at liberty to strike or thrust him and endanger the breaking of his arm, or the taking away of his sword by that grip.

2. If you are both crossed in the close fight upon the bastard guardant ward low, you may put your left hand on the outside of his sword at the back of his hand, near or at the hilt of his sword arm and take him on the inside of that arm with your hand, above his elbow is best, and draw him in towards you

---

[38] A word of caution: In grounds 1 and 2 Silver describes techniques where you *'endanger to break his arm'*. Silver is quite correct in this assertion and consequently you or your training partner *will* know when you've got the grip correct. You have been warned.

strongly, wresting his knuckles downward and his elbow upwards so may you endanger to break his arm, or cast him down, or to wrest his sword out of his hand, and go free yourself.

3. In like sort upon this kind of close, you may clap your left hand upon the wrist of his sword arm, holding it strongly and therewith thrust him hard from you, and presently you may thrust him in the body with your sword for in that instant he can neither ward, strike, nor thrust.

4. If he strike home at the left side of your head, and there withal come in to take the close or grip of your hilt or sword arm with his left hand, first ward his blow guardant, and be sure to put in your left hand under your sword and take hold on the outside of his left hand, arm or sleeve, putting your hand under the wrist of his arm with the top of your fingers upward, and your thumb and knuckles downward, then pluck him strongly towards your left side, so shall you indirect his feet, turning his left shoulder toward you, upon which instant you may strike or thrust him with your sword and fly out safe, for his feet being indirected, although he have his sword at liberty, yet shall he be not able to make any offensive fight against you because his time will be too long to direct his feet again to use his sword in due time.

5. Also if he attempt to close or grip with you upon his bastard guardant ward, then cross his sword with the like ward, and as he comes in with his feet you have the time of your hand and body, whereby with your left hand or arm you may put by his sword blade, which thing you must suddenly and strongly do, casting it towards your left side, so may you uncross and thrust him in the body with your sword and fly out instantly, for if you stay there he will direct his sword again and endanger you, this may safely be done, or you may uncross and turn your point up, and strike him on the head, and fly out instantly.

6. If he presses in to the half-sword upon a forehand ward, then strike a sound blow at the left side of his head turning strongly your hand and hilt pressing down his sword hand and arm strongly, and strike your hilt full in his face, bearing your hilt strongly upon him, for your hand being uppermost you have the advantage in that grip, for so may you break his face with your hilt, and strike up his heels with your left foot, and throw him a great fall, all this may safely be done by reason that he is weak in his coming in by that moving of his feet, and you repel him in the fullness of your strength, as appears in the chapter

of the short single sword fight, in the 23rd ground of the same.[39]

7. Remember that you never attempt the close nor grip but look to his slip, consider what is said in the 8th general rule in the second chapter, and also in the 26th ground of the single sword fight in the 4th chapter.

---

[39] This technique particularly impressed Matthey, who says in the introduction to his 1898 edition, *'whereas many a man can do much damage to his opponent after being run through the body... few if any would be able to stand up against a back-handed blow in the face with the pommel of a regulation sword.'*

CHAPTER 7

Of the short sword and dagger fight against the like weapon

1. Observe at these weapons the former rules, defend with your sword and not with your dagger, yet you may cross his sword with your dagger, if you may conveniently reach the same therewith, without putting in of your foot, only by bending in of your body, otherwise your time will be too long, and his time will be sufficient to displace his own, so that you shall not hit it with your dagger, and so he may make a thrust upon you, this time that I here mean, of putting by of his sword is, when he lies out spent[40] with his sword point towards you, and not else, which thing if you can do without putting in of your foot, then you may use your dagger, and strike strongly and suddenly his sword point therewith up, or down, to indirect the same, that done, instantly therewith strike or thrust at him with your sword.

2. Also you may put by his sword blade with your dagger when your swords are crossed, either above at forehand ward, or

---

[40] The position of a weapon at the end of an offensive action with the arm extended. The force of the attack 'lies spent'.

below at the bastard guardant ward and therewith instantly strike or thrust with your sword and fly out according to your governors, of this you may see more at large in the chapter of the single sword fight in the 24th ground of the same.

3. Also if he is so foolhardy to come to the close, then you may guard with your sword and stab with your dagger, and fly out safe, which thing you may do because his time is too long by the number of his feet, and you have but the swift time of your hand to use, and he cannot stab till he has settled into his feet[41], and so his time is too late to endanger you or to defend himself.

4. Know that if you defend yourself with your dagger in the other sort than is afore said, you shall be endangered to be hurt, because the space of your dagger will be still too wide to defend both blow and thrust for lack of circumference as the buckler has.

5. Also note when you defend blow and thrust with your sword, you have a nearer course to offend your enemy with your sword than when you ward with your dagger, for then you may for the most part from your ward strike or thrust him.

---

[41] He cannot launch a secondary attack with his dagger until he has finished pressing in with his first attack.

6. You must neither close nor come to the grip at these weapons, unless it is by the slow motion or disorder of your adversary, yet if he attempts the close, or to come to the grip with you, then you may safely close and hurt him with your dagger or buckler and go free yourself, but fly out according to your governors and thereby you shall put him from his attempted close, but see you stay not at any time within distance, but in due time fly back or hazard to be hurt, because the swift motion of the hand being within distance will deceive the eye, whereby you shall not be able to judge in due time to make a true ward, of this you may see more in the chapter of the backsword fight [Chapter 4] in the 12th ground of the same.[42]

7. If he extends forth his dagger hand you may make your fight the same, remembering to keep your distance and to fly back according to your governors.

    Every fight and ward with these weapons, made out of any kind of fight, must be made and done according as is taught in the backsword fight, but only that the dagger must be used as is above said, instead of the grip.

---

[42] This expands on advice given in ground 3.

8. If he lie bent[43] upon his Stocata with his sword or rapier point behind his dagger so you cannot reach the same without putting in your foot, then make all your fight at his dagger hand, ever remembering your governors, and then if he draw in his dagger hand, so that you may cross his sword blade with yours, then make narrow space upon him with your point and suddenly and strongly strike or bear his point towards his right side, indirecting the same, and instantly strike or thrust him on the head, face arm or body, and fly back therewith out of distance still remembering your governors.[44]

9. If he lies spent upon his variable fight then keep your distance and make your space narrow upon him, till you may cross his sword or rapier point with your sword point, whereupon, you having won or gained the place, strike or thrust instantly.

10. If he lies bent or spent upon the Imbrocata bear up your point, and make your space narrow and do the like.

---

[43] The position of a weapon before an offensive action is initiated. This is the swordsman's equivalent of a cocked gun.
[44] The strike or thrust is made with the sword, not the dagger.

CHAPTER 8

Of the short sword and dagger fight against the long sword[45] and dagger or long rapier[46] and poniard

1. If you have the short sword and dagger, defend with your
    sword and not with your dagger, except you have a gauntlet or
    hilt upon your dagger hand, then you may ward upon forehand
    ward, upon the double[47] with the point of your sword towards
    his face.

---

[45] Not to be confused with the two-handed medieval *longsword*, this refers
rather to a single handed sword of 'imperfect length'. Silver objects to this
longer sword because they are *'too long by almost half a foot to uncross,
without going back with the feet, within distance or perfectly to strike or
thrust within the half or quarter sword.' Paradoxes of Defence* Chapter 15

[46] *Paradoxes of Defence* is not only critical of the thrust centric Italian
fencing system, but also damning of the rapier as a weapon. In the
Dedicatory to *Paradoxes* Silver says; *'...when the battles are joined, and
come to the charge, there is no room for them to draw their bird-spits, and
when they have them, what can they do with them? Can they pierce his
corselet with the point? Can they unlace his helmet, unbuckle his armour,
hew asunder their pikes with a Stocata, a reversa, a Dritta, a Stramason, or
other such like tempestuous terms? No, these toys are fit for children, not
for men, for straggling boys of the camp, to murder poultry, not for men of
honour to try the battle with their foes. '* This chapter, therefore, is
important as within the techniques described Silver seeks to prove the
superiority of the short sword over a weapon that he so despised.

[47] That is to say that you can ward with your sword and dagger
simultaneously, providing that you have hand protection.

2. Lie not aloft with your short sword if he lies low variable upon the Stocata or Passata, etc., for then your space will be too wide to make a true cross in due time, or too far in his course to make your space narrow, which space take heed to make very narrow, yes, so that if it touches his blade, it is better.

3. I say make your space narrow until you can cross his sword blade strongly and suddenly, so shall you put by his point out of the right line, and instantly strike or thrust, and slip back according to your governors.

    But take heed unless you can surely and safely cross go not in, but although you can so cross, and thereupon you enter in, stay not by it but fly out according to your governors.[48]

4. If with his long sword or rapier he charge you aloft out of his open or true guardant fight, striking at the right side of your head, if you have a gauntlet or closed hilt upon your dagger hand, then ward it double with forehand ward, bearing your sword hilt to ward your right shoulder, with your knuckles upward and your sword point toward the right side of his breast or shoulder, crossing your dagger on your sword blade, resting it there upon the higher side of your sword bearing

---

[48] You are only to press in if you can first safely indirect you opponent's blade.

both your hilts close together with your dagger hilt a little behind your sword bearing both your hands right out together spent or very near spent when you ward his blow, meeting him so upon your ward that his blow may light at your half sword or within, so that his blade may slide from your sword and rest with your dagger, at which instant time thrust forth your point at his breast and fly out instantly, so shall you continually endanger him and go safe yourself.

5. If he strike aloft at the left side of your head, ward as aforesaid, bearing your sword hilt towards your left shoulder with your knuckles downward, and your sword point toward the left side of his breast or shoulder, bowing your body and head a little towards him, and remember to bear your ward to both sides that he strike you not upon the head, then upon his blow meet his sword as aforesaid with your dagger crossed over your sword blade as before , and when his sword by reason of his blow upon your sword shall slide down and rest upon your dagger, then suddenly cast his sword blade out toward your left side with your dagger, to indirect his point, and therewith thrust at his breast from your ward and fly out instantly, the like may you do if his sword glance out from yours, upon his blow.

All this may safely be done with the short sword and closed hilted dagger or gauntlet.

6. Stay not within distance of the long sword or rapier with your short sword, nor suffer him to win the place of you, but either cross his sword, or make your space very narrow to cross it before his blow or thrust be in force, yet keeping your distance whereby he shall strike or thrust at nothing, and so shall be subject to the time of your hand against the time of his feet.

7. Keep distance and lie as you think best for your ease and safety, yet so that you may strike, thrust or ward, and when you find his point certain, then make your space narrow and cross his sword, so shall you be the first mover, and enter first into your action, and he being an after doer, is not able to avoid your cross, nor narrow space, nor any such offense as shall be put in execution against him.

8. Having crossed his long sword or rapier with your short sword blade, and put his point out of the straight line by force then strike or thrust at him with your sword and fly out instantly according to your governors.

9. Stand not upon guardant fight only, for so he will greatly endanger you out of his other fights because you have made

yourself a certain mark to him, for in continuing in that fight only you shall not only weary yourself, but do also exclude yourself from the benefit of the open, variable, and closed fights, and so shall he have four fights to your one, as you may see in the chapter of the short single sword fight in the 15th ground thereof.

10. If he lie in open or true guardant fight, then you may upon your open and guardant fight safely bring yourself to the half sword, and then you may thrust him in the body, under his guard or sword when he bears it guardant, because he is too weak in his guard, but fly out instantly, and he cannot bring in his point to hurt you except he go back with his foot or feet, which time is too long to answer the swift time of the hand.

   If he put down his sword lower to defend that thrust then will his head be open, so that you may strike him on the head over his sword and fly out therewith, which thing he cannot defend, because his space is too wide to put up his blade in due time to make a true ward for the same.

11. Understand that the whole sum of the long rapier fight is either upon the Stocata, Passata, Imbrocata, or Mountanta, all these, and all the rest of their devices you may safely prevent by keeping your distance, because thereby you shall still drive

him to use the time of his feet, whereby you shall still prevent him of the true place, and therefore he cannot in due time make any of these fights offensive upon you by reason that the number of his feet will still be too great, so that he shall still use the slow time of his feet to the swift time of your hand, and therefore you may safely defend yourself and offend him.

Now you plainly see how to prevent all these, but for the better example note this, whereas I say by keeping of distance some may object that then the rapier man will come in by degrees with such ward as shall best like him, and drive back the sword man continually, to whom I answer, that he cannot do, by reason that the sword man's traverses are made circular wise, so that the rapier man in his coming in has no place to carry the point of his rapier, in due time to make home his fight, but that still his rapier will lie within the compass of the time of the sword man's hand, to make a true cross upon him, the which cross being made with force he may safely uncross, and hurt the rapier man in the arm, head, face or body, with blow or thrust, and fly out safe before he shall have time to direct his point again to make his thrust upon the sword man.

12. If the rapier man lies upon the Stocata, first make your space narrow with your short sword, and take heed that he strikes

not down your sword point with his dagger and so jump in and hurt you with the thrust of his long rapier, which thing he may do because he have commanded your sword, and so you are left open and discovered and left only unto the uncertain ward of your dagger, which ward is to single for a man to venture his life on, which if you miss to perform never so little you are hurt or slain.

13. To prevent this danger you must remember your governors, and presently upon his least motion be sure of your distance, and your narrow space, then do as follows.

14. If he lies upon his Stocata, with his rapier point within or behind his dagger hand out straight, then lie you variable in measure with your right foot before and your sword point out directly forth with your space very narrow as near his rapier point as you may, betwixt his rapier point and his dagger hand, from which you may suddenly with a wrist blow, lift up your point and strike him on the outside or inside of his dagger hand, and fly out withal, then make your space narrow as before, then if he thrust home at you, you are ready prepared for his thrust, or you may thrust at his dagger hand, do which you shall think best, but your blow must be only by moving your wrist, for if you lift up your hand and arm to fetch a large blow then your time will be too long, and your space too wide

in due time to make a true ward to defend yourself from his thrust, so shall you hurt him although he has a gauntlet thereon, for your thrust will run up between his fingers, and your blow will cut off the fingers of his gauntlet, for he cannot defend himself from one blow or thrust of twenty, by reason that you have the place to reach home at his hand, and for that cause he cannot prevent it, neither can he reach home to you without putting in his foot or feet, because the distance is too large, but upon every blow or thrust that you make at his hand slip back a little, so you shall still upon every blow or thrust that you make at him, be out of his reach.

But if upon your blow or thrust he will enter in with his foot or feet to make home his Stocata or thrust upon you, then by reason of you sliding back, you shall be prepared in due time to make a perfect ward to defend yourself with your sword.

Therefore ever respect his rapier point and remember to make and keep narrow space upon it with your sword point, that you may be sure to break his thrust before it be in full force.

15. If he thrust at your higher parts with his point a little mounted, then make narrow your space with your point upon his, if you cross his blade on the inside between his rapier and his dagger,

if he presses in then from your cross beat or bear back his point strongly towards his right side, and having indirected his point, strike him on the inside of the rapier or dagger hand or arm, or on the head, face, or body, and fly out instantly.

Or you may upon his pressing in with his thrust slip your point down as he comes in, and put up your hilt and ward it guardant, and therewith from that ward cast out his point, and suddenly strike him in one of the places aforesaid, and fly out instantly remembering your governors.

16. If he lies fast and does not come in, then strike and thrust at his dagger hand, with your wrist blow and slip back therewith every time.

17. But if he lies fast and beat down your point with his dagger, and then thrusts at you from his Stocata then turn up your hilt with your knuckles upward and your nails downward, taking his blade upon the backside of yours towards your left side and bear it guardant toward that side, and so may you offend him as before is said upon that ward.

18. The like may you do upon him if he lie out with his point, when you have crossed the same with yours, and then strike it to

either side, and so indirect his point, and then strike or thrust and fly out.

19. The like must you do, if he lie with his point direct toward your belly.

20. But if you cross his point so mounted or directed as above said, upon the outside of your sword with his point a little higher than your hilt, so that you may cross his blade, then if he thrust over your blade single uncrossing the same, then you may break it with your forehand ward out towards your right side, and if he comes in therewith, then strike him on the outside of his rapier hand or arm, or on the head or face, and fly out therewith.

21. But if he thrusts in over your sword as above said and press in his blade strongly double with the help of his dagger, then put down your point and turn up your hilt guardant, so shall you safely defend it bearing it guardant out toward your left side and from that strike him in between his rapier and dagger in one of the aforesaid places, and fly out.

But if from the cross he slip his point down to thrust under your sword, then strike down his point toward his left foot and therewith strike him on the outside of his rapier hand or arm, head, face, or body and fly out instantly, according to your governors.

Also you may upon this of his point down, then turn your point short over his blade in your stepping back, and put your point down in the inside of his blade, turning up your hilt guardant as aforesaid, and then if he thrusts at you, bear it guardant towards your left side, and then have you the same offensive blows and thrusts against him as is above said upon the same ward.

22. If he lie after the Stocata with his point down toward your foot, then cross his blade on the outside, and if he turn his point over your blade to make his thrust upon you, then turn up your hilt and bear it guardant as above said, bearing it out toward your left side, and from that ward offend him as aforesaid.

23. Also in this fight take heed that he thrusts you not in the sword hand or arm, therefore ever respect to draw it back in due time, remembering therein your twofold governors, in your coming in, to make your cross or narrow space.

24. If at sword and dagger or buckler he strikes in at the outside of your right leg ward it with the back of your sword, carrying your point down, bearing you knuckles downward and your

nails upward, bearing your sword out strongly toward your right side, upon which ward, you may strike him on the outside of the left leg, or thrust him in the thigh or belly.

25. The like may you do if he strike at your other side, if you ward his blow with the edge of your sword your hand and knuckles as aforesaid, casting out his sword blade toward your left side, this may be used at short or long sword fight.

26. You must never use any fight against the long rapier and dagger with your short sword but the variable fight, because your space will be too wide and your time too long, to defend or offend in due time.

27. Also you must use very large distance ever, because out of that fight you can hardly make a true cross because being within distance, the eye is deceived to it in due time.

28. Remember in putting forth your sword point to make your space narrow, when he lies upon his Stocata, or any thrust, you must hold the handle thereof as it were along your hand, resting the pommel thereof in the hollow part of the middle of the heel of your hand toward the wrist, and the former part of the handle must be held betwixt the forefinger and thumb, without the middle joint of the forefinger toward the top

thereof, holding that finger something straight out gripping round your handle with your other three fingers, and laying your thumb straight out upon the handle, so shall you lay your point out straight toward his, the better to be able to perform this action perfectly, for if you grip your handle close over-thwart in your hand, then can you not lay your point straight upon his to make your space narrow, but that your point will still lie too wide to do the same in due time, and this is the best way to hold your sword in all kind of variable fight.

29. But upon your guardant or open fight then hold it with full gripping it in your hand, and not laying your thumb along the handle, as some use, then shall you never be able strongly to ward a strong blow.

30. This have I written out of mine entire love that I bear to my countrymen, wishing them yet once again to follow the truth, and to fly the vain imperfect rapier fight, the better to save themselves from wounds and slaughter, for who so attains to the perfection of this true fight which I have here set forth in these my *Brief Instructions*, and also in my *Paradoxes of Defence*, shall not only defend themselves, but shall thereby bring those that fight upon that imperfect fight of the rapier

under their mercy, or else put them in Cobb's traverse[49], where of you may read in the 38th chapter of my *Paradoxes* aforesaid.

---

[49] *Cobb's Traverse* – to run away. Silver tells us that, '*This Cobb was a great quarreller, and did delight in great bravery to give foul words to his betters, and would not refuse to go into the field to fight with any man, and when he came into the field, would draw his sword to fight, for he was sure by the cunning of his traverse, not to be hurt by any man. For at any time finding himself overmatched would suddenly turn his back and run away with such swiftness, that it was thought a good horse would scarce take him. And this when I was a young man, was very much spoken of by many gentlemen of the Inns of the Court, and was called Cobb's Traverse and those that had seen any go back too fast in his fight, would say, he did tread Cobb's Traverse.*'

CHAPTER 9

Of the sword and buckler fight

Sword and buckler fight, and sword and dagger fight are all one, saving that you may safely defend both blow and thrust, single with your buckler only, and in like sort you may safely ward both blows and thrusts double, that is with sword and buckler together which is a great advantage against the sword and dagger, etc., and is the surest fight of all short weapons.[50]

---

[50] The advantages of the sword and buckler fight over the sword and dagger fight are discussed at length in *Paradoxes of Defence* Chapter 24. *'The dagger is an imperfect ward, although borne out straight, to make the space narrow, whereby a little moving of the hand, may be sufficient to save both sides of the head, or to break the trust form the face or body, yet for lack of the circumference his hand will lie too high or too low, or too weak, to defend both blow and thrust. If he lie straight with a narrow space, which is to break the thrust, then he lies too weak, and too low to defend his head from a strong blow. If he lie high, that is strong to defend his head, but then his space will be too wide to break the thrust from his body. The dagger serves well at length to put by a thrust, and at the half sword to cross the sword blade, to drive out the agent, and put him in danger of his life, and safely in any of these two actions defend himself. But the buckler, by reason of his circumference and weight, being well carried, defends safely in all times and places, whether it be at the point, half sword, the head body, and face, from all manner of blows and thrusts whatsoever, yet I have heard many hold opinion, that the sword and dagger has the advantage of the sword and buckler, at the close, by reason*

of the length and point of the dagger, and at the point of the sword, they can better see to ward than with a buckler. But I never knew any, that won the close with the dagger upon the sword and buckler, but did with himself out again. For distance being broken, judgement fails, for lack of time to judge, and the eye is deceived by the swift motion of the hand, and for lack of true space with the dagger hand, which cannot be otherwise, for lack of circumference to defend both blow and thrust, it is impossible for lack of true space in just time, the agent having gotten the true place, to defend one thrust or blow of a hundred. And it is most certain, whosoever closes with sword and dagger against the sword and buckler, is in great danger to be slain. Likewise at the point within distance, if he stand to defend both blow and thrust with his dagger, for lack of true space and distance, if he has the best eye of any man, and could see perfectly, which way the thrust or blow comes, and when it comes, as it is not to deny that he may, yet his space being too large, it helps him nothing, because one man's hand being as swift as another man's hand, both being within distance, he that strikes or thrusts, hurts the warder.'

CHAPTER 10

Of the two hand sword fight against the like weapon [51]

These weapons are to be used in the fight as the short staff, if both play upon double and single hand, at the two hand sword, the long sword[52] has the advantage if the weight thereof is not too heavy for his strength that has it, but if both play only upon double hand, then his blade which is convenient length agreeing with his stature that has it, which is according with the length of the measure of his single sword blade, has the advantage of the sword that is too long for the stature of the contrary party, because he that can cross and

---

[51] The two hand sword, sometimes referred to as a great sword, had developed from the medieval longsword and had it's heyday during the late 15th and early 16th centuries. The weight and length of these weapons could vary greatly, but a sword in excess of 5' and weighing between 6-8lbs would not be unusual. Due to this increased length and weight their handling was closer to pole weapons than to their medieval forebears. By the late 16th early century the two hand sword had become obsolete as a weapon of war but would still be played at public feats of arms into the 17th century. As a weapon Silver thought very highly of the two hand sword, stating in *Paradoxes of Defence*, chapter 21, that '*The two hand sword has the advantage against the sword and target, the sword and buckler, the sword and dagger, or the rapier and poniard*'.

[52] The longer blade

uncross, strike and thrust, close and grip in shorter time than the other can.[53]

---

[53] This is a slight modification to the statement given in *Paradoxes of Defence* that the perfect length of a blade for a two hand sword '*be the length of the blade of your single sword*'. While this still holds true if both protagonists only wield their swords two handed, and for the same reasons that Silver gives for the short sword being superior to the long sword, he adds here that if both fight single and double handed then the longer blade has the advantage. See Chapter 11 ground 1.

CHAPTER 11

Of the short staff fight, being of convenient length, against the like weapon[54]

The short staff has four wards, that is two with the point up, and two with the point down.

1. At these weapons ever lie so you may be able to thrust single[55] and double, and to ward, strike, or thrust in due time, so shall your enemy, if he fights only upon double hand be driven of necessity, seeking to win the place, to gain you the place whereby you may safely hurt him, and go free yourself by

---

[54] Silver's short staff would more commonly be called today a 'quarterstaff'. The convenient length for a short staff, half pike, forest bill, partisan or glaive is described in Chapter 19 of *Paradoxes of Defence*, '*...stand upright, holding the staff upright close by your body, with your left hand, reaching with your right hand your staff as high as you can, and then allow to that length a space to set both your hands, when you come to fight, wherein you may conveniently strike, thrust, and ward, and that is the just length to be made according to your stature.*' This works out at roughly between 8' and 9' in length. The staff would normally be shod with a sharp steel tip at either end; hence it's other common name the 'tip staff'. Silver says '*The short staff is most commonly the best weapon of all other... by reason of his nimbleness and swift motions, and is not much inferior to the forest bill.*'

[55] A single handed thrust using your left/rear hand. This gives you around a 1' extra reach.

reason of your distance, and where you shall seek to win the place upon him he shall not be able to gain the place upon you, nor keep the place from you whereby he shall either be hurt, or in great danger of hurt, by reason of your large reach, true place and distance, your fight being truly handled keeping itself from close and grip.

2. And in like sort shall it be between two, which shall play upon the best, that is, if they play both double and single handed.

3. If you find yourself too strong for your adversary in any manner of ward, whether the same be above or below, put by his staff with force, and then strike or thrust him from it.

4. But if you find him too strong for you upon his blows from aloft, so that you can hardly bear them upon your ward, then when he strikes in aloft at your head, and by his main strength would beat down your staff, and so give you a hurt before you shall be able to come again into your ward, against such a one give the slip in the sort, suddenly draw back the higher part of your body a little and your foremost foot withal, and slip in the point of your staff under his staff, and thrust single at him, and fly out withal, so shall you be sure to hit him and go out free.

5. If he lie aloft with his staff, then lie you with your back hand low, with your point up towards his staff, making your space narrow because you may cross his staff to ward his blow before it come into full force, and then strongly and suddenly indirect his point, and so thrust at him single, the which you may do before he can remove his feet, by reason of the swiftness of your hand and fly out therewith, do this for both sides of the head if cause requires it, so shall you save both your head, body, and all parts, for your upper parts are guarded, and your lower parts too far out of his reach.

6. If he lie low with his point down, then lie you with your point down also, with your foremost hand low and your hind most hand high, so that you may cross his staff, and do all things as is said in the other.

7. If he lie upon the thrust then you lie with your space narrow lying up or down with your point in such sort as you may cross his staff, and thereby you shall be able to put or beat by his thrust before it is in full force, and then strike or thrust, ever remembering your governors.

If upon this any will object that if this be true, then it is in vain to strike, or thrust, because he that does it is still in danger, this doubt is answered in the short single sword fight, in the 12th ground thereof.

8. If your adversary strike aloft at any side of your head or body, ward it with your point up and making your space so narrow that you may cross his staff before it comes in full force bearing or beating down his blow strongly, back again towards that side that he strikes in at you, and out of that ward, then instantly, either strike from that ward turning back your staff, and strike him on that side of the that is next to your staff.

Or lift up your staff again, and so strike him on the head or body, or thrust at his body double or single, as you may find your best advantage ever in holding your staff, let there be such convenient space between your hands, wherein you shall find yourself most apt to ward, strike or thrust to your best liking.

9. If you play with your staff with your left hand before and your right hand back behind[56], as many men find themselves most apt when that hand is before, and if your adversary upon his blow come in to take the close of you, when you find his staff crossed with yours near his hand, then suddenly slip up you

---

[56] Left handed

right hand close to the hind side of your foremost hand, and presently loosing your foremost hand and put in under your own staff, and then cross or put by his staff therewith and with your hand take hold of his staff in such sort that your little finger be towards the point of his staff, and your thumb and forefinger towards his hands, and presently with your right hand mount the point of your own staff casting the point thereof over your right shoulder, with your knuckles downwards, and your nails upwards, and so stab him in the body or face with the hind end of your staff, but be sure to stab him at his coming in, whether you catch his staff or not, for sometimes his staff will lie to far out that upon his coming in you cannot reach it, then catch that arm in his coming in which he shall first put forth within your reach, but be sure to stab, for his staff can do you no hurt, and having so done, if you find yourself too strong for him, strike up his heels, if too weak fly out.

10. The like must you do if you play with your right hand and your left hand back behind[57], but that you need not to slide forth your left hand, because your right hand is in the right place of your staff already to use in that action, but then you must

---

[57] Right handed

displace your left hand to take hold of his staff, or the grip as is aforesaid, and to use the stab as is above said.

11. If both lie aloft as aforesaid, and play with the left hand before, if he strikes at the right side of your head or body then must you cross his staff before his blow is in full force, by making your space narrow, and then strike it strongly back again towards his left side, and from that ward you may turn back your staff and strike him backward therewith on the left side of his head, or lift up your staff and strike him on the right or left side of the head, body, or arm, or thrust him in the body, the like blows or thrusts any you make at him whether he strikes or thrusts, having put by his staff, remembering your governors.

The like order must you use in playing with the right hand before.

12. But if he thrust at you continually then ever have a special care to consider, whether he lie aloft or below, and do continually thrust at you therefrom, then look that you ever lie so that you make your space so narrow upon him, that you are sure to cross his staff with yours, and put it before it is in full force, and from that ward, thrust at him single or double as you find it best, and if he remember not to fly back at that instant when

he thrusts it will be too late for him to avoid any thrust that you shall make at him.

CHAPTER 12

Of the short staff fight against the long staff[58]

1. If you have a staff of the convenient length against a staff of
    longer length than is convenient, then make your space
    narrow, and seek not to offend until you have strongly and
    swiftly put by his point which you shall with ease accomplish,
    by reason of your narrow space and your force, then strike or
    thrust him as you shall think best.

2. This short staff fight against the long staff is done in the same
    sort that short staff fight to short staff fight is done, but that
    the man with the short staff must always remember to keep
    narrow space upon the long staff, where so ever the long staff
    shall lie, high or low, continually make your space narrow upon
    him, so shall you be sure if he strikes or thrusts at you, to take
    the same before it be into its full force and by reason that your

---

[58] The long staff measured somewhere in the region of 12'–18'. Silver says,
'*The short staff hath the vantage of the long staff and morris pike in his
strength and narrowness of space in his four wards of defence.*' (*Paradoxes
of Defence* Chapter 27) The exception to this rule is when fighting at night
when the longer staves '*boldly make home their fights, and if need be
against desperate men, that will venture themselves to run in, they redeem
their lost times. But the other with the shorter weapons for lack of light,
can make no true defence.*' (*Paradoxes of Defence* Chapter 29).

force is more with your short staff than his can be at the point of his long staff, you shall cast his staff so far out of the straight line with your short staff, that you may safely enter in with your feet, and strike or thrust home at him.

3. Yet this present shift he has at that instant, he may slip back his staff in his hands, which time is swifter then your feet coming forward, whereby he will have his staff as short as yours, yet by reason that at the first you cast his staff so far out of the right line, that you had time to enter with your feet[59], you shall then be so near him, that you make narrow space upon him again, so that he shall have no time to slip forward his staff again in his former place, nor go back with his feet, and so to recover the hind end of his staff again, because if he slip forth his staff to strike or thrust at you, that may you safely defend because of your narrow space upon him, and therewithal you may strike or thrust him from your ward, either at single or double.

4. But if he will go back with his feet thinking by that means to recover the whole length of his staff again, that can he not do in convenient time because the time of your hand is swifter

---

[59] Do not enter within distance until you have cast the long staff's point aside otherwise the long-staff man may thrust at you as you come in.

than the time of his feet, by reason whereof you may strike or thrust him in his going back.

5. Again it is to be remembered in that time that you keep him at bay, upon the drawing in of his staff, the hind end thereof lying so far back behind will be so troublesome for him, that he can make no perfect fight against you and commonly in his drawing in of his staff it will be too short to make a true fight against you, neither to offend you or make himself safe.

6. If he attempts the close with you then stab him with the hind end of your staff as said in the fight of the two short staves of convenient length, in the 9th ground thereof.

NOTE: Remember that at the morris pike, forest bill, long staff and two handed sword, that you lie in such sort upon your wards that you may both ward, strike and thrust both double and single, and then return to your former wards slips and lying again and then are you as you were before.

The like fight is to be used with the javelin, partisan, halberd, black bill, battle axe, glaive, half pike, etc.[60]

---

[60] These polearm weapons are not mentioned elsewhere in *Brief Instructions* but are described in *Paradoxes of Defence*. The halberd, black bill and battle axe all measure between 5'-6' in length '*and may not be*

used much longer, because of their weights'. Silver considers them to have the advantage over all swords single or double. The partisan, glaive and half pike are 'weapons of perfect length' and have the same advantages as the short staff and forest bill. The javelin is similar in length to the long staff or morris pike.

92

CHAPTER 13

Of the fight of the forest bill against the like weapon and against

the staff[61]

1. The forest bill have the fight of the staff but that it has four
    wards more with the head of the bill[62], that is one to bear it
    upwards, another to beat it downwards so that the carriage of
    your bill head is with the edge neither up nor down but
    sideways.

    The other two wards are one to cast his bill head downwards
    towards the right side, and the other towards the left.

    And upon either one of these wards or catches run up to his
    hands with the head of your bill[63] and then by reason that you
    have put his staff out of the right line, you may catch at his

---

[61] The forest bill is a hafted billhook, often with the addition of a thrusting
spike, the stave being the same length as a short staff (8'-9' long). Silver
says *'The Welsh hook or forest bill has advantage against all manner of
weapons whatsoever.'* (*Paradoxes of Defence* Chapter 21)
[62] The forest bill has eight wards in total. The first four wards are the same
as the short staff, that is to say warding on the stave behind the weapon's
head as discussed in ground 9. The next four wards with the head of the
weapon utilize its weight and ability to hook.
[63] Presumably you run the bill head up to your opponent's hands along the
haft of their weapon, effectively pinning it while you attack.

head, neck, arm or legs, etc., with the edge of your bill, and hook or pluck him strongly to you and fly out withal.

2.   If you cast his staff so far out that your bill slides not up to his hands, then you may safely run in sliding your hands within one yard of the head of your bill, and so with your bill in one hand take him by the leg with the blade of your bill and pluck him to you and with your other hand defend yourself from his grips if he offers to grapple with you.

3.   If you fight bill to bill do the like in all respects as with the staff in your fight, for your bill fight and staff fight is all one, but only for the defence and offence with the head of the bill, and where the staff man upon the close if he uses the stab with the butt end of his staff, the bill man at that time is to use the catch at the leg with the edge of his bill in the second ground above is said.

4.   Remember ever in all your fight with this weapon to make your space narrow whether it is against the staff or bill so that whatsoever he shall do against you, you shall still make your ward before he is in his full force to offend you.

5.   Also if you can reach within the head of his bill with the head of your bill then suddenly with the head of your bill snatch his

bill head strongly towards you, and therewithal indirect his bill head and forcibly run up your bill head to his hands, so have you the like advantage as above said, whereas I spoke of running up towards his hands.

6. If he lie low with this bill head then if you can put your bill head in over the head of his bill, and strongly put down his bill staff with your bill head, bearing it flat, then you may presently run up your bill head single handed to his hands and fly out therewith, so shall you hurt him in the hand and go free yourself.

7. The like may you do with your bill against the short staff you can press it down in the like sort, but if he has a long staff then run up double handed with both hands upon your bill, which thing you may safely do because you are in your strength and have taken him in the weak part of his staff.

8. If he lie high with his bill head then put up your bill head under his and cast out his bill to the side that you shall find fittest, so have you the advantage to thrust or hook at him and fly out.

Or if you cast his bill far out of the right line then run in and take him by the leg with the edge of your bill, as is said in the 2nd ground of this chapter.

9. If you ward his blow with the bill staff within your bill head then answer him as with the short staff.

NOTE: That as the bill man's advantage is to take the staff with the head of the bill so that the staff man by reason that the head of the bill is a fair mark has the advantage of him in the casting aside of the head of the bill with his staff or beating it aside, the which if the bill man look not very well into it the staff man thereupon will take all manner of advantages of the staff fight against him.

CHAPTER 14

Of the fight with the morris pike against the like weapon[64]

1. If you fight with your enemy having both morris pikes with both points of your pikes forwards, low upon the ground, holding he butt end of the pike in one hand single[65] with knuckles upwards and the thumb underneath, with the thumb and forefinger towards your face and the little finger towards the point of the pike, bearing the butt end of the pike from the one side to the other right before the face, then lie you with your arm spent and your body open with your hand to your right side with your knuckles downwards and your nails upwards.

---

[64] A pike of this period could be anywhere between 12'-18' long and in less than two decades after Silver's death it would sadly become the iconic weapon of the English Civil War. In the 15th and 16th centuries pike formations were a common sight on European battlefields, most famously used by Swiss mercenaries and German *Landsknechts*, although English armies of this period tended towards shorter polearms. Given this context the name *morris pike* is curious. Morris is commonly thought to mean *Moorish*, derived from Morisco (Spanish), the same etymological root as in *morris dancing*. One proposed explanation for this name is that the ash staves, or even the weapons themselves, were imported from Spain, for which there is some evidence. However, this is far from a consensus view.
[65] The rear/left hand.

Or you may lie in that sort, with your hand over to the left side with your knuckles upwards and your nails downwards, whereby all your body will be open. If then he shall suddenly raise up the point of his pike with his other hand and come thrust at you, then in the mounting of his point or his coming in, suddenly toss up the point of your pike with your hand single and so thrust him in the legs with your pike and fly out therewith.

Or else you may stand upon your ward and not toss up your point but break his thrust by crossing the point of his pike with the middle of your pike by casting up your hand, with the butt end of your pike above your head, and so bearing over his point with your staff, to the other side as for example.

2. If you lie with your hand spent towards the left side of your body, then suddenly bear his point over strongly towards your right side.

    If you lie with your hand spent towards your right side then bear his point towards your left side, and thereupon gather up your pike with your other hand and thrust him and fly out.

3. If he continue his fight with his point above, and you lie with your pike breast high and higher with you hand and point so, that you make your thrust at his face or body with your point directly towards his face, holding your pike with both your hands on your staff your hind hand with your knuckles upwards and your foremost hand with your knuckles downwards and there shaking your pike and falsing at his face with your point as near his face as you may, then suddenly make out your thrust single handed at his face and fly out withal, which thrust he can hardly break one of twenty by reason that you made your space so narrow upon his guard, so that you being first in your action he will still be too late in his defence to defend himself.

4. But note while you lie falsing to deceive him look well to your legs that he in the meantime toss not up the point of his pike single handed and hurt you therewith in the shins.

5. If he lie so with his point up aloft as you do then make your space narrow mounting your point a little and cross his pike with yours and strongly and suddenly cast his point out of the right line and thrust home from the same single or double as you find your best advantage, and fly out therewith.

Or you may run in when you have cast out his point sliding both your hands on your staff till you come within three quarters of a yard of the head of your pike and stab him therewith with one hand and with your other hand keep him off from the grip.

6. Now if he be a man of skill, notwithstanding the making of the fault in suffering you to do so yet this help he has, as you are coming in he will suddenly draw in his pike point and fly back withal, then have you no help but to fly out instantly to the middle of your pike and from thence back to the end and then are you as at the first beginning of your fight you were.

7. If you find that he lie far out of the right line with his point or that you can so far indirect the same then cast your pike out of your hands, cross over upon the middle of his pike, by which means you shall entangle his pike, then while he does strive to get his pike at liberty, run you in suddenly drawing your dagger and strike or stab at him.

8. Then if he has the perfection of this fight as well as you, he will be ready with his dagger as you are with yours, then must you fight it out at the single dagger fight as is shown in the 15th chapter: then he that has not the perfection of that fight goes to wrack.

9. And here note that in all the course of my teaching of these my brief instructions if both the parties have the full perfection of the true fight then the one will not be able to hurt the other at what perfect weapon so ever.

10. But if a man that has the perfection of fight shall fight with one that has it not then must that unskilful man go to wrack and the other go free.

CHAPTER 15

Of the single dagger fight against the like weapon

1. First know that to this weapon there belongs no wards nor grips but against such a one as is foolhardy and will suffer himself to have a full stab in the face or body or hazard the giving of another, then against him you may use your left hand in throwing him aside or strike up his heels after you have stabbed him.

2. In this dagger fight, you must use continual motion so shall he not be able to put you to the close or grip, because your continual motion disappoints him of his true place, and the more fierce he is in running in, the sooner he gains you the place, whereby he is wounded, and you not anything the rather endangered.

3. The manner of handling your continual motion is this, keep out of distance and strike or thrust at his hand, arm, face or body, that shall press upon you, and if he defend blow or thrust with his dagger make your blow or thrust at his hand.

4. If he comes in with his left leg forward or with the right, do you strike at that part as soon as it shall be within reach, remembering that you use continual motion in your progression and regression according to your twofold governors.

5. Although the dagger fight be thought a very dangerous fight by reason of the shortness and singleness thereof, yet the fight thereof being handled as is aforesaid, is as safe and as defensive as is the fight of any other weapon, this ends my brief instructions.

Finis.

Printed in Great Britain
by Amazon

63588380R00079